THE ANIMAL INDOORS

CARLY INGHRAM

AUTUMN
HOUSE PRESS

Pittsburgh, PA

"Autumn House Press" and "Autumn House" are registered trademarks owned by Autumn House Press, a nonprofit corporation whose mission is the publication and promotion of poetry and other fine literature.

This project is supported in part by the National Endowment for the Arts.

Autumn House Press receives state arts funding support through a grant from the Pennsylvania Council on the Arts, a state agency funded by the Commonwealth of Pennsylvania, and the National Endowment for the Arts, a federal agency.

Cover art by Elana Engelman-Lado
Cover design by Melissa Dias-Mandoly

ISBN: 9781938769870
LCCN: 2021939701

The delineation of the people over against every other thing that constitutes the general ecosystem is problematic in ways that already bear what's problematic inside.

—FRED MOTEN

TABLE OF CONTENTS

ASSURED ENVIRONMENTS

Do the fields grow
up from your shoulders
in the wet wet earth.
Last night, I held skin
for the first time, and it was not
pretty. The pumpkin patch is filled
with diamonds, but we don't care.
The trash is spilling over from our yard,
but we don't care. I envy
the good bones in the garden.
The labor in the many
unseen places. It is unlikely
for the current situation to proceed
like this. Suddenly listening is less
of a knife. The locks to the outside
doors are placed on each of our heavens
but loosely, like wetted hair.
What I'm trying to understand
is when I look at fear,
I know she is not there.
But when I turn back,
all of the blood armies have fences,
all the tiled knives have doors,
and all of my selves are buried
inside the nonliving sea.

DISAPPEARING INTO A FICTION

*

The totals keep flinching
out their plastic bags
and it ain't too much bother
no more to capture
ur whole booty out the bag.
Ur Crock-Pot can make summer.
Ur tamed animal can say all the things
we wished to say to each other
in those moments
we made up for loss.
So alone in the pink summer-stunk
sky. So alone in the political
ribcage. So alone in the hot,
saturated blood.

*

The disordered person seeks
health daily only to find old
dew settled in each pocket square.
The habit of taking
started young. Make yourself
better and self-help are raging
in the mosh pits. No time
for maps. I'm looking for something
to worship. A thing like pity
is so small in the hands of a saint.
A sinner is so small when I look
at what is done. How can I fix
any of the desires of my heart.
I pant for cherishing. Whose
wrongdoing is weeping now.

*

We sit in humid acknowledgment
of rage rage rage rage rage.
To kneel is to have peace
with the savior. Cathedral hair cathedral body
cathedral tongue all gathered together
in unison in unison. Asking which key which key.
By praise we mean telepathy, which is different
than how pennies sit their whole lives
along a roundtable of non-discussion.
Flat water at the top, and the penny sinking
like smashing a stick of butter inside
the mouth and waiting for the effect
to settle. How curious to begin again.

*

The concert lights are neon-green like holy T-shirts
or paper trees. Once in a tunnel, I found
out how to grip onto something so hard you lose
your sense of place. *I want that old thing back*
like driving so far the name for sunflower disappears.
The only resolute answer to panting
is discovering what was lost. There was a bushel
of something more vibrant
than nostalgia stepping on wings of diamonds,
pure light like zeal or the plague.
At last, I picked the right gem.
It was circular but real real clear.

IRREVERSIBLY FUCKED IT UP

The correct answer
is that the tide rises and falls,
and at the shore, you can go
and sorta relax, pretend you're
just looking and wetting your toes,
not even defining anything. These
race conversations keep getting
worse and worse. The answer to fixing
the brown problem is not yelling
directions. School is not the answer,
my teacher. We already know how
to live. Just give us an in, let us in
to your homes, to your institutions,
to your minds. Stop saying *how do
I*, when we both see the red sun
and know what blood
can make us pay for.

FOR A MOMENT, EVERYTHING IS SMALL
AND FAMILIAR

*

I put on my yelling cheetah shirt
and the Miami tailgate guy says *wanna fuck*.
The room is loud, lifting us
out of our chairs and onto the playing field.
I follow the stairs with my eyes
like they are gonna take me
somewhere just by looking.
I am remembering where I got
those cutoff jean shorts I had on.
I took them from a friend I thought was gorgeous,
not sexually, just like physically formed by wealth
and generous flowers. I had sprayed my hair,
labored with the curling iron, and dark lined my eyes.
I had no hair except on my pussy,
which was always my little secret.
I thought about what would happen
if someone opened my panties and found
I wasn't a woman the way I should be.

I liked the thought of letting
my leg hairs grow out so long I could braid them,
watching them sway in a river
as I sat shoeless. Now, I'm on a flat
of green beside the water. I met her there.
She swept her hair away from her face,
and I swam through the freshness in her eyes.
I knew her name though she never said it.
We were rolling through the dirt,
hands in each other's hair, and her body
became the orchard all around.

*

In the freezer aisle at Costco,
I ran into a homosexual
wearing a steadfast floral crown.
It looked like the plastic Kmart
flowers I smelled in October
after not quite getting over her.
The scouters for the TV shows
people watch to outlive themselves
came up to me, and I began
to audition. The part began
as a role for a super dyke
and turned into a role for
a femme wearing lace-up
boots. The homosexual passing
by us in the store knew me well
from other auditions and passing
time posted up in each other's
souls and calling ourselves the names
of oceans and drainage companies.
We be spilling over and out.
The terms and conditions for the show
were written on a river's path. We went
outside to walk the path. At first
eating up the steps I felt myself
still the owner, but soon I felt myself
moving quite without knowing
yesterday was not beginning.

*

Even the gold chains must go to sleep
as they hang their fate underground.
Each vendor's face holding the same worn-in
you look hungry, are you hungry look.
I leave the visions of gold a bit hysterical
and enter a night of loud karaoke.
The girl on stage is a regular. She has trendy bangs
and stained teeth and is glamorous
in the way only sadness can be.
The curve of wanting stuns me.
I cannot go beyond it. I keep passing by
the underground gold chains, laughing
at the bulk of the need. How erosion shines.
The karaoke singer begins sobbing tears of rain
and water, blowing like autumn.
I do not think to chase love into her body
with my hand or even to look her way.
I think only of her eyes squinting at the heavy stage light,
angry at the weight of her limbs.

WHITE TIGERS

Forever is the same thing as white tigers.
Du-rags dripping plain jewels at sunset.

It is easier to ask many things of a stranger
than of a brother. White tiger, I will miss you

in the next sunset. Regrettably, I'm no good
at forgiveness or many kinds of goodness.

I have my white tiger to play with
in the dark. After making a small mound,

I smooth it down, smash it, rather, and begin to dig
afresh, until I can put the capsule I've prepared

inside. The white tiger is waiting on hands and knees
ready to enter, as though it has already eaten

the hole many times, made it while asleep,
continually providing fresh bedding.

White tiger, white tiger, who are you,
I beg. Tell me your name,

to whom do you belong, can I destroy
you all at once or only by degrees.

Tell me how to destroy you.
White tiger, I need you to make the final blow.

PRAISE POEM

I keep borrowing
your hands, each finger
reaching out towards
the opal stool.
It will survive;
love will survive.

WHAT SORT OF ANIMAL ARE YOU

All the women were washing at the creek, at the sink, at the large communal basin at the center of town. Walking on, hands tied behind their backs in bushy sleeves, they did not have an answer to the question.

Still at the tailgate, the man asks, *what part of me do you secretly dress in each day*. The cat lady next door is sad about loving and bruises. About stones and wolves. The collected news in a warm-weathered, republican wastebasket.

We enemy the crowds,
· borrowing each belief
we solidly consume.

THE DETRIMENTAL YEARS OF BECOMING A YOUNG WOMAN

Like the baldest eagle, we stare straight into the sun.
Raise a hand to the devil. But it's not a matter
of whose country anymore. There is
stamina in anger and blood.

Half the reason for the celebration
was to put the legs up on the chairs:
for the act, for the holiness, for the saved.
On a billboard, crossing into a new city,

the dancing emoji girl appeared, except
she was real and really dancing in fur boots
with caged sparkles. Just the right size.
I slipped the girl a flyer I received

from a stranger. It said: notice, getting ripped
off the billboard is easy. Just ask the power
how to come about erasing yourself. Ask them
if you might be removed. Ask them for something

to cleanse you. After reading the flyer, she practiced
the motions nightly, and even in the light, the trim
of her skirt stayed red. I stick the painted marbles inside
the cardboard, and as it gently tilts, they color a slurred speech.

The language of a single loaf. I stand above it,
amazed at the conspirator of motion.

NATURE ADAPTED TO LIVE ON THE ROCK

Inside the hut, the man with dirty
boots is on a chair, picking apart
leaves to make a cigar. We watch
as the product is being made.
On the long ride to Viñales, we see
wet wind going by us through the window,
and someone in the car is asking
why not diversify the economy.

I was interested in this idea as it does
or does not pertain to plagues.
The simple gesture of a holy war
or attributing a whole illness to a name.
Like the plenty of a large-mouthed soup
the poor keep feeding on their hunger.
Why do the people keep popping out
their heads to look from their homes.
I don't know, but I know there's romance
in looking out. The painted walls
and the man standing as tall as a horse.

THIS WOMAN'S WORK

Black Lady Gaga

She's clawing cavity
through the ambidextrous night,
singing personhood into existence.
Round chandeliers hang from her ears,
lighting up the bathroom clearing—
the space between opulence
and regular canned soup.
She installs a new seamstress
into her fingertips' knowledge.
Together, they place diamonds
around the webs of spiders
who they glare at in envy
for having been born without
being so attached to the spaces
without life. In a bath of black paint,
she finds a square of bare tub
and begins to pray: Oh delicious
mother of the heavens, please rein
in your most incomplete fire
on us all. Might we never again
be without the black paint (our fire)
the words in the stone, the charcoal
in the bats. The rhythm in the unwritten
voices—how softly they speak. *Speak.*

An ode to Simone Biles's hair

My grandma's silver-blue hair is installed
in crashing curls, breaking off into little universes.
Before the store was opened, she pearlized the products
on her counter, by counting them backwards and forwards,
and repeating the ritual until she's quite full. In all the ads,
Simone shows up as a bad bitch with a serious problem.
Feral as a tongue, the way her image felt
to the stands watching the hair in a ponytail,
not tight, not fixed, flying up at the edges.
If only more things would fly up at the edges

and refuse to agree. When the Wi-Fi at the Taco Bell
is lit in the middle of the night and the clearing
in the mind keeps whispering *gimme gimme more.*
And her hair spoke directly to each heaven
when it said *but I love Zac Efron*
so much I might Postmates him,
I mean Venmo him, for his love tonight.

A table full of glass Cardi Bs

The collectors' yop sounding off
inside the historical art museum.
The Cardi glass objects are installed
on a wooden table between a wall
of descriptive words and a mural
with strange bulging proportions.
In this installation it is OK to touch
the exhibit. Feel free to go up
and press ur fingers upon
the glass. When touched, the glass
releases a small sound, a yelp,
but with the signature Cardi noise
still attached. When a man touches
it, it's different. Instead of a yelp,
a really cute horny sound echoes back,
accompanied by a small squirt
of water meant to mirror
love and its residual effects.
How its sudden claim can call
upon a person to feel very new,
wet even, abundant even. Startled
into existence, again.

The Real Housewives of Atlanta *in the recording booth*

We don't do classical
unless bae puts it on says A.
I think I've been here before
in Italy, in a cocoon—it's a rare

procedure that helps sterilize
the eyelids by tightening
the pussy-strings. *Pass the mic*
says R. to the producer, to herself,
to anyone. *Have you ever taken off*
your neon lights at night, gotten into
something really sterile and warm,
and tried to take a bite out of yourself.
A. messes with the Auto-Tune
and replies within the effect **bite me*
bite me, bitch I'm tasty*. T. was quite
bored so she called the trap gods,
and they conveyed the message to her
that in fact she was tastier than all
these bitches and A.'s man would agree.
The producer started in with the hook.
A. picked up her pocket mirror
and thick-whispered *imma big boss*
made of broken glass like museum Atlantis.
I'm such a boss when I look in the mirror
I can still see the sharp edges of the beautiful object
I can still see my smile, the lips.

Jordyn Woods on the moon

I've never been Black
on the moon. I've never seen
her curves so up close, her body
so pale and not wanting a photo.
I've never been sitting beside a whole
moon, staring silently without a photo.
I've never held Jesus beside a pale
moon or said their face was gorgeous.
I've never wanted to be a moon
until I was so close
to it. New moon, new me.
I've never known myself
to be a woman with pride
until I was undressed

by the moon
and could not let go,
could not let go, kept
my fingers sealed
across my secret.
I'm not supposed to be here,
to be here naked
in this dark body.

NOT EATING WAS MY SUPERPOWER

It was an essential trip, a day letting salt out on the party plates.
I did not have on an elegant gown, but the fantasy did exist.
In the well-lit, ecstatic room, he asked me to sit down.
To which I did not reply but found myself sitting.
The news was he had found the contents of his heart somewhere
beside me and had to share. He pulled some of the flowers from the wall,
there were flowers all around us, tangled and intrusive.
Started saying I was connected to everything, the flowers on the wall,
the very place we sat, the lines and lines of homeless people
standing outside, waiting for a meal, even without outlasting the day.
Move with me he said, I have to go to Baltimore, new start, build
something. He looked at the flowers carefully flinging
their bodies and said, *it's OK, I can protect you*, fed me a loose
petal from the floor. Like the time a stranger asked for a kiss
just by pointing to their face. And I made myself into a yes
without any courage or wanting. I am realizing I never see
women take off their hats and dance for money on the train,
so I make her in my mind, as I would anything beautiful.
The woman peels off her shirt, the tattoo lines on a map.
She warns everyone that they are safe and to please move over.
Falling to the ground with purpose, she twists one leg over
the other, shuffling her feet back and forth.
In court, they ask about her audience, but nobody saw
if she was harmed that night. Small sweat like elastic as she holds
out the hat from her head, knowing she is worth anything at all,
depending on who's watching. Next time, in the stadium
she woos the crowd with a bipartisan number sent direct postage
from the officials. Next time, the routine might be permanent.
Bright white flowers, ecclesiastical and alive.

YOU'LL BE OK

After Tao Lin

*

I don't think saying *you'll be OK* helps.
You have to keep at it and enforce it.
If it's you, then you fix yourself
and look in the mirror to fix your hair.
Look back at wrongs done via Venmo.
I say *I'm making you sad*
even if I'm sad and you are
smiling out loud at laundry folds.
The world, all the things around me,
are still not good. What if I stay in bed.

*

I haven't seen you in a while. Last night,
I thought about us walking by a dance club
and looking in, but not going. In my mind
we went in and it was red dancing.
I took your hand in mine. Then I realized
it wasn't your hand, you had left. So I went out
into the night, called your name, and thought of love.
    I send you curated birthday emojis.
    I save your box of cigarettes from the trash.
    Three a.m. message—*let's hang at the park. I like hugs.*

*

The identity of you, seamless as a corset.
Like the pebbles at the bottom of a fishbowl, we sink
into each other's shallowness. Not that I *want it*—
are you ready and willing and miss you. The scam calls
and pop-up ads and miss you. The officer
I don't know at the phone number bar, who stares
with Midwest eyes, and miss you.
The parked van menu items miss you,
three-for-one misses you. Pull on her hand
and desire will slap you in the face,
awake. Knock on her door
and she will have
no rooms left.

OF NO SPECIFIC LIGHT

After Kevin Young

I am hoping to go to the ocean
and fish your head out of the sea.

Your head is like an ambient noise,
wading like a purpose to drown.

The throwing was the best part,
how I claimed a severed thing as mine.

Then all at once, you're mine—
     Put me down.

Every curve of forgetting. We were made to forget.
We were made to wear our shame like an ocean.

After I've secured you from the sea,
I put the teeth on a gold chain: a collection

is better than a singular event. A *chain* of events
or its beginning, how it started.

When I think of the waves, I want mercy.

FOR THEY WILL INHERIT THE KINGDOM

The bundles/ the bundles of light/ under your eye-shirt/
undo me/ your eye-shirt, the one you wear
as a crown/ lifts my head from the pews/ our sight
no longer lingers/ on the exit row/ so we seat
ourselves alone/ alone the unbuttoned version/ of our crownless
selves/ ourself/ ourself, the crownless
community./ I take a seat on the wooden bench/ the limbs
so mobile in their sockets/ I pull a limb past
its limit/ out its door/ limb-door/ place a limit
on memory/ I place a limit on memory/ I don't repeat the name
of/ spilled edges of water/ glass
figurines all lined up/ I venture towards
forever/ like it's meant to be./ It's
memorized already/ just do it again/ forever is always
the same./ The first cave takes us into an alleyway/
where we pause just to look around./
The heat has lifted by now/ but we can still feel our belongings/
close by, near our hearts./ I'm fully awake now,
looking straight into the heart/
of spring./ The sale is still on,
so we are minding our business,/ uncovering
what's necessary./ The price tags
sometimes require/ a little lifting or digging/ I impale
a piece of grass at the corner by the fire hydrant/ and find
its worth. Next, the dirt waves/ its price tag
right by my hand/ as I'm lifting
it away from my grass/ and so naturally, I discover
its worth./ As I'm moving the dirt
back in position/ the tag on my hands
starts getting agitated/ in the wind,
and the sun begins/ to hang down the truth of
its numbers./ I look to the sun to find
its worth./ While it's looking away, I bury
my worth/ right there, right there, in the dirt.
I make/ I make a painted shell/ in the corner
of the room/ the room
the room is clear/ the boy at the party says/
where he's from they paint the shells
of hermit crabs/ but were I to imagine

its cage/ it wouldn't be farther than my country/
in the blue water, you can see blue fish/
the demonstrators making
noise/ a sympathetic touch/ I paint it all silent./ Listen
listen listen./ An insistence
to or towards/ what has already been
insisted upon/ it shows the way
forward/ implicit bias/ it tells you
what to think/ how to behave/ what it look like/
what it sound like/ *how* to create space/ what a space
is/ who is in the space/ and you can feel it move
even if you aren't sure of what it is/ you can feel how
it might create open eyes on the boardwalk/ bodies still.

TIMELESS OARS

Once, on a trip toward
the health we most desired,
we came across the barren
hot springs. If you've ever seen
a mountain path, you already know
the way I'm speaking of.
Angel on the shoulder, demon
in the wind, and each time we steal
a stray crop from the path it turns
us on so much, we bury it immediately.

In the first psalm I learned without the words,
it says *let the father practice
anger*. In the decisive room, he bears
a wooden spoon to each child's
backside. What do you mean
of pleasure. I've forgotten how
I found the hot spring, whether
when we say damage, what we mean is—
parking the car outside the motel hot spring
and running so hard all the faces disappear.

SAVE YOU

The black freedom struggle
is the indigenous peoples'
struggle. Is women's struggle
is queer people's struggle
is pertinent to yt dads
who wear hats and yt
moms who sell jewelry
is not a fact of mattering
is a fact of survival. Is
the struggle of the self
and selfhood, or personhood
and existence. Cannot
be separated from you
or me from you or me.
Is, in fact, a living breathing
entity, is in fact a people,
a wind, a breath so big
it might counter thunder
or ask something so heavy
of us, we bow to the earth.
Wind is a breeze, is a chatter,
is a letting go, is me and you vibing
in every season. All the shadows
look exact in their waves now.
Whirlpools and Big Mac salad
mighty warriors with small teeth.
What's the biology of resistance.
Ain't polite policy, ain't nothing
we heard before.

JUST LAY THERE FLAT

Two people push a cart full of churros
through the busy halls of the subway
station. They push the sugar
up the sloping ramp like they are prepared
to receive something once they stop.
As I take the churro from her brown hands,
I imagine that I am her daughter. She says
finish everything on your plate, my love,
remember always your manners.
I taste the fried dough like an angel puffing
a dime bag. The flimsy paper barely holds
the churro up like the thin walls between
my face and my image. How I look and do not see.
When it's time to go home, she packs up the cart
in the same way she wheeled it through the halls
before. It will be late now and she'll have some leftover.
Like purpose is her sack of belongings,
she'll place them on her back and walk.
She is happy to be home
and wash her hands of the cinnamon.
I ask her for a lemon tea,
and she puts a small braid in my hair.

LAST NIGHT I SAW A BOAT JUST AS IT WAS EXITING MY PURVIEW

The birth canal, the spirit, the self.
A moment's moment. A tally's tally. A fish's fish.
A feast for its sake. A mother for its birth, its time.
The indecency of it all. And crime, our markings on flesh.
The bad of us pulled out in lingering restraints
Even farther. The catapult from bad to everlasting.
And small fingers on top of a boat's lifting sail.
The night ride with wind and our tongues out lapping
Without noise. Pure air beside our boat
As time hit us steadily without feeling.
The movements become clear when we see them
Catching up just now to the scissoring fear of pretending
I was meant to be in this place
With my shoes off and hair down, unrestrained
And feigning listening. I am the roundabout story
From yesterday about the bears that will not harm
Without cause. So often I can make time
For casting out stones from my shelves
And wiping the dust into new places.
I don't care for these dungeons
The way I used to. The way I used to
Look all dressed up in lace, and patchwork,
Long or short sleeves, buttons undone
And my flesh, it was red and knowing and green
And new and abundant and except for that one
Time, I didn't love you, I didn't love at all.

FRANK OCEAN'S "IVY"

She stands outside our apartment in Manhattan, is making images for us to hang on the wall above our couch. Exact sketches of live performances, a lady in all glitter reciting poems and then Moses Sumney hits the stage all a cappella and face covered. After nobody comes to my party, she sits on the apartment floor and recites a black-and-white photograph. It's like a love we've seen before but didn't realize until we woke up somewhere new. Outside, her shapes beg realization in the night, listening to the spaces between our words. The seashell she gave me the night we were in love, and the way she looks at Kendrick in a stadium full of people leaving. She writes an exact time in Frank Ocean's "Ivy" on a Post-it. I tried to post it on my skin and keep walking, but it kept falling off. I blame the culture I blame the mirror I blame my hands. I want to be a bag of water: I want us to both be poured into a single bag. How you like to ditch the earth with its cellphones and mountains and touch nothing. I went to go pee beside the merch stand and you went to pee too and I thought maybe I'd lost you because we'd gone in separate stalls, but you knew we'd both walk back outside on the night grass and look for each other.

I FEEL DIRTY TODAY

The antique store sells carpets
with old-sounding names and feels
pretty. The train car was all windows
until it was not, and the hills were
far beyond our eyes. On the church steps,
a man is swaddled in a cheetah blanket,
his human eyes visible to the whole world.
When the voices of the earth converge
into a single voice, all I can hear is the noise
coming through: *People who really want*
to pull themselves off the streets.
You know how a person makes
you feel is what matters. He already got
a liter of juice, don't give him anything.
The funny thing, she says, *is Fox News*
began as a business.

When the baby was floating
down the biblical river,
we tried to look away, but the curve
of her body was so intimate
as it climbed its individual
cage back to the point we all begin.
The sponge daddy with its yellow
smiling face. Its infertile course
from smiling production to smiling
isle to smiling home.
On the stem of a flower,
there's a shoot of exact green.
On the run from we the people
we do not know but wear proudly and liberally.
The photographs people give away
are always of blank noise:
two normal-looking people staring
straight ahead.

EVERY GIRL WANTS A PINK SKY

Like sitting down on pine straw
crumbling the legs to pumping.

Yellow sky, like the time in a painted-van
in Austin, in Illinois, in Redding. The memory

of smooth portraits drawn to size.
The couple holding the park portrait

is from out of town, pressing the shape
of their temporary mouths to dine-out

straws. Bundles and bundles of leaning
recipe books at home without the wars

of anything spilled across their faces.
On Independence Day, you might find

them stored away on a boat's water
holding out an umbrella for the sun

almost touching the immigrants'
earth with their eyes.

ANIMAL PRINT

The wrong lily frogs
lace Ziplocs and cracked
pepper on the table.
Find the love everywhere.
South seasons' universal
voice, universal noise.
What is freedom is not
here. The big man's
puffy charade sitcom.
Famous slideshows of fat
to thin people make me
masturbate internally.
Tell us more about getting
better. Tell us what better
is, how to claim
the cages we've
lost to American lives:
cages in the bedroom,
the kitchen, cages
at the border. For the
fountain to speak, it must
be ill. It must be ill.

PRAISE POEM

The dog through the window walks unashamed,
moving to consume the love nearest by.
Pushing their head infinitely to the stranger,
not fearing the talking sun. A flea walks up
to my cup and floats as if on ice
hovering above, on, above. I push it away,
and it flickers into the air. Just yesterday, I saw
a woman give a visitor a handful of fruit.
Going into her kitchen, there were persimmons
and tangerines on the counter, lemons tarrying on the floor,
nothing living in the rightful container.
Their hands were so heavy they had to push them together
to hold it all. The window dog is much like
the Tinder dogs is much like a screen playing fire.
I know the men are good because they are near
the dogs. I know the fire is good
because I've felt alone without.
The day I moved to LA I saved the plane ticket from home.
It's sentimental to imagine another monochromatic lifetime.
Still, I have memory to place her foothold in meaning.
Moten says *the settler is not someone who goes to someplace*
that's not their own the settler is someone who goes someplace
and tries to make it their own. If ownership, then reconstructive
surgery. The store I'm in, or this world, keeps asking
if I want my receipt. A prescient child's hand
holding an acorn. I have no need for innocence.
It's becoming less hard to imagine the dignity
of standing up and leaving a seat empty for someone new.

WHAT DOES THE ARK YOU'RE INSIDE LOOK LIKE

A straggler is stationed at the curb
of the fat tourist restaurant, sucking
the bones of corn dry.
Down the street, a free hand
drops a coin purse out the window
at a little laughing girl.
And when the floodlight
comes down with the heavens,
she is singing like ecstasy
flooding straight from the bones.
For sale! For sale! For sale!
A pale-yellow dress strays quietly
beside the bird hopping pleasantly
in its cage. Four years working
at the hotel washing dishes.
Three years in a row coming
to bring stuff to the poor country.
Gaps on gaps on
whose fault on
political lines on
the names of blame.
White fragility and a handwoven cloth.
The long boat ride to paradise
like snails appearing on the earth.

THAT WHICH CARRIES BREATH OR THE
LIVING WIND

There was a bushel of something vibrant:
large palm fronds wanting the care of the day.
We put up shelves, lifted the things with time.
The model room helps plan our very future.
I found a lock without a key and hid
her body far away from my knowledge.
At the edge of an ice rink, the stranger
stands firm as any real prison with guards.
A few careless patients fall down again
from the stairs to the window, out the wall.
Absently, the light was new, was newer.
We are placing the shelves full of ourselves
like a candle knocking over a dove.
Already the old room has lost its praise.

Already the old room has lost its praise.
There was a horse running down a mountain,
a mountain in the sea. The horse paused to
look around and saw a projection of
itself across the waves. As it began
to see. To see the animal move, it
joined in with itself. With itself, it
was moving freely. The mountain was
inside a small valley where a quiet
family lives, and when they small talk, it
sounds like the drip of a faucet. I'm not
trying to say living is easy, it's
not. Easy is the horse as it's drowning.
The habit of my taking started young.

The habit of my taking started young.
Each child is perfect and untamed but
we name them, each one. The checkout man at
Whole Foods said *you listen to rap/ Yeah* I
said/ *u know Nipsey Hussle/ yeah* I said/
He died he said/ *how* I said/ he laughs, I
guess because I should have known/ *shot* he said.

If you google *how did Nipsey Hussle*
these are the results: *meet Lauren London,*
get famous, die, make his money. This begs
the question which one would you fuck which one
would you marry which kill. Fuck the woman,
marry the money, and by that point, you
don't gotta pick kill because the news dropped.

Don't gotta pick kill because the news dropped
and he dead. You pretend you can pick kill
but each time kill pick you, it pick you and
then it follow you around like a god-
damn drama queen just following around,
littering on the ground, eating your food.
In science, we asked the kids what happens
when any car collides/ the student said
when cop cars collide/ the teacher said *what/*
the student said *cop cars/* when you ask the
kids a question they'll repeat the whole thing
back with the wrong verbs and the wrong subjects
so even if *them is hungry,* I can't
unsee the old reality I saw.

Unsee the old reality I saw
while entering the record store mostly
looking for that song I already know.
It plays on a loop, in an actual
circle visually, I can see it.
It goes *let's begin again.* And the notes
are pretty remedial. A warm soup
going down. I'm in the DMV with
all the people of color off Flatbush.
The man next to me talking endlessly
about some science I never heard of.
And the numbers keep coming as if the
people were numbers as if the people
were numbers. And suddenly! The people

were numbers. And suddenly! The people
are numbers. The pr*sident shows up on the TV.
He's bein' a big boss and shouting his
hands like they are catching flies. One time I
asked you how you like it, slow or fast. In
the hallway we act like everything
is an embarking. From here to there and
back. If the pr*sident were a number he would be
multiplication or its opposite.
You said you like it like frozen ice, the
kind where only the top has been frozen
over and just below, the very cold
water sits, waiting. We can't help but flail
our own arms out in peace for resistance.

We can't help but flail our own arms out in
peace for resistance. And what if my
worst fear does come true. I'm in the middle
of a ditch and the earth holds nothing.
Being nowhere near the groups and groups of
people on their way to the falls.
Our history, we are
represented by the walls
painted with myths of our own histories,
myths we learn that sprout weeds
which may continue to make life.

That we all may live
in harmony amen.

RETWEET

Lately, all the names
are hers. All the sounds
are hers. She looks out
the window and I bask
in her heat, a puppy
still feeding from its mother.
I owe so much to the world
these days. She says *have
grace*—and I think she means
something like vision. See
it for what it is. Not what is
really there. The wet snow
crunching and the ice that makes
its way into our homes
by accident. Watching
it melt like a secret birth
or a memory kept tight
in a frame.

AMERICA SELF-STORAGE

One time I was brave
like any giants' expectations.
Ultra-unscented police
and the sunset in reflection.
A music video with strings
rehearsing for a final note.
Next time I travel
it'll be to the stove
or your new mailing address;
the thing I still own of yours.
Any person I belong to
screams to the bush.
When it screams back
some people can extend
their limbs and just relax.
For example, do you see
that angel floating in an inner tube.
Now see that other one.
Which one can evaporate
as slow light hitting its edge.
We are standing by succulents,
eating Chipwiches, and I want
your body closer to mine,
want to hear your sudden fall from grace
when the traffic lights change
and I grip your hand with sweat
and wild glee. The scissors
in your purse casting stones
on bright water. Do not.

RIGHTEOUS VIOLENCE

In a picture on the train there's a flower bigger than a head. And the dark face is sipping from the flower like a bee, caressing it for safekeeping with her face. After applying lipstick, she carefully undresses an orange, pulsing a small sliver to scent the room. In the photo, she sees herself in the mirror *objects in mirror are closer than they appear*. In the mirror, there are stained glass pews and wooden saints surrounding. As she walks down the cathedral aisle, she's holding a flower larger than her face. She doesn't stumble but I might have imagined she did. She was going straight towards the elders—not ancestors—just old people standing at the front with no flowers. They had the unique position of capturing the flowers and giving back a thumbnail square of liquid. Her closed legs saw the stand of hanging gold chains. She didn't want gold like the powerful, she wanted it like the weak.

A DARKNESS INVENTED BY THIRST

Even us, the burden we carry in taupe woods.
Two people can enter the shoe store
at a time. The clock is counting down to see
how quick you can get the pair. The fake rain
forest surrounds the people looking
for the pair. There are sounds of rain
and raffle tickets offering inseminated
trust and sunlight lamps. Two people wait—
all shadows in sleeping bags outside the store
—until the risen moment when time enchants
and one must enter. Walking one pace
in front of the other, be sure to pressure
the waters at the correct height
weight and jar. Once boiled, take a look
at the flesh. Again, measure the distance
from the highlighted route to the pair.
If on the highway at night, do not
slow down at any cost. The problem
with pain is it's not temporal. It only begins.

BAD CHARACTERS

I love fake hitting
the person I love.
Charm bracelets
in a catalog sale.
Round table
with painted fruit.
The individual
indoor trash can
soon a fleet outside.
Even the names
in a song become
the characters
in our buttoned-up hearts.
Next time I love, I'll
love lawn chairs
under the overhang,
the wet grass nearby
with a bug stalking
its heels. Even in time,
we are living wrong.
All the stolen
goods out of place
now. Even the ones
we hold close. What
do you mean of pleasure.
We've climbed onto the veranda
and sang our truest aching.
The bad characters'
redeeming quality
is a dollar store with missing
lights. What letter can I bring
back to life.

COMPETITION: THE REVISIONIST SAND

I get into bed into bed
with supremacy. The election
is on for this day the red and blue
the red and blue. Fastly, we market thyself.
Only the human bones
pulled apart each one from their
meat-strings. Intestines flung down
walls like holiday decor. No, not
the beasts again. Not desire. Not
in this home. We pray to a god
that heals, like anything goes these days.
I see a long current, the size of a voice.
Your tallest chair at the edge
of your seat, and not yelling out.
VCRs cast about the dust shop like
a medium making space for other
voices. Worn-out sneakers quill
as broken-air whistles.
Drawstring and insta-press voices.
Combing the bristles of a voice. Hearing
the sexual gestalt. The sudden waste.
Whose. Whose. Whose. Whose. Whose.
The voice, a clearing. *Like anything goes
these days* is a revisionist history.
Begging now, through
breath-stained glass, you say
*cut her. She is the sun. Bleed
the sun, bleed her, I cannot see.*

THE REVOLUTION IS EDIBLE

Each time the personhood
     nears its edge.
A hometown so dear
     you can smell
its insides, the very prosperous
     names of creation.
How many places have you
     traveled. And when
you return, what is it like.
     The bears still learn
from their young how
     to tame a thing.
Flatbush is the ghetto part,
     our driver responds to a question
we didn't ask. Can you spare
     some affluence. The soil is being patted down
into place by sharp elegant hands.
     The urgency of *the times*
is on my desktop, laptop, TV.
     A special meditation in diversion.
Can't finish saying what I was saying
     before because I got too many plastic bags now.
More than ever, I can imagine wasting
     you by degrees: the sudden violence
of dry earth rising up in rain.
     At first, I could not claim even myself as hate
even as I baptized myself in her waters.

RECOVER FROM WHATEVER

Sad sad sad sad sad sad flowers
asking *which key, which key.*
The elderly city
lights photograph themselves
directly. In the entryway,
there's so much space
between a life that's still loading.
Down the sidewalk, a baby rocking
on the ground, not in a home.
Too many Sams do weapons
and keep safe journals
about highly effective habits.
The dailiness of food and sleep.
My hate finds me sterile,
panting at the ghost.
Normal couples everywhere.

JUST HAVING FUN

I'm looking directly into the eyes of strangers
to find the least common enemy. My eyes
are always wide-open like the stage.
Where in the world is walk around the planted thing
and come back earlier than expected.
We clamor as though those in need
of water can sense its edge.
Young nights, carouseling the parking lots
looking for garbage we could claim.
Rap-thick and sewn-in or tied-down
and bone-legged, we settle the bets
on us by handing you your change with a smile.
Where in the world is undress my coat,
dissolve this back. Early baby in the stomach
a picture ready to be seen. Motherhood
like shopping on discount for a partner.
You alright, baby? You alright, baby?
Girls with their names in fake gold
across their chests, the cursive path
to personhood. Waiting on someone
to place them beside the gold, on a scale,
and let the weight of it be seen.

THE INFINITELY EFFICIENT BODY

How do you become like famous
like really good at instantly being
a solid color.

Old people cover their furniture
with plastic for protection.
Young people stay over with their toes out.

As though your own wallet could hold
the ticket we need to get in.
The mesmerizing piece of rinsing

is the sound of preparation.
A child asked me what the ticket was for.
Easy clothes and your hair down.

Laugh while looking at the moon.
Then you can have a stone and place it
anywhere where grass will not grow wild.

AND SO, WE GOT TO BE FOR EACH OTHER
WHAT THE OTHER MISSED

Shifting to the edge, she lifts off the stool
her whole weight taking up the hall
as she passes by framed collections.
The slender breasts in the frame flittering
in blank air as if solo and unmarked.
My love is not a question of the dominant.

A woman tells me she's dominant
and I imagine her crossed on a stool
coming at me like a shy devil, unmarked
by beauty. As I pass her in the hall
I notice her veil lift for a moment, flittering
as if it could ready itself for collections.

After some years curating art collections
she holidays at a villa with the dominant
field-members. On the gulf, hem flittering
white, as the ground supports like a stool.
The edges of makeup sweating a thin hall
down her face. My kiss leaves her unmarked.

We hopped a fence, entered an unmarked
area not meant for travelers or collections
of time. The woman I love is down the hall,
and I leap over the alarm's dominant
sound. Together, we press into a stool,
knowing we cannot get full, air flittering.

It is easy to erase her into a flittering
image. Any love is our love if unmarked
by the sense of staying on the round stool
for a while. Setting payroll in collections.
Even after we are together, the dominant
plea I have is framing you in my hall.

I hang the picture of my love in the hall.
She is an America, her edges flittering
in the small light. There is no dominant
reason for me to make love unmarked
in the dark. Except that my collections
are always near, hollow bodies in a stool.

We know the dominant lover is unmarked.
She lays still in the hall, eyes flittering
to the collections, foreseeing a lover in a stool.

TRIVIA

Did you know jealousy was a time before us.
We snowsuit and Tostito our way into the future.
The romantics, flinging their salt shakers, said
they do it for love. We walk into the exhibit,
knowing love has come upon us: the toy cars
zipping around their mini lanes, chasing
to the stoplights' edge, jamming up
(time time) and circling back around.
All of their love is spilling over us now.
The railing outside our historical museum
scares us into seeing leaves and sky and air.
As the clotting continues, beautiful and beautiful
days sway and then tilt. An infection of the mind
is still holding the people, as I might conjure them.
Industry and her smooth legs, her pear-shaped filters,
her loving arms, and how she bounce that ass up and down.

LISTENING

Have you ever fixed the mind
everything you hear the far-off noises/
everything your mind is not.
One narrow little channel.
Listen you will change/ within you.
A change without your volition.
Insight/ as you are not only
everything, all those distant to me
also. You will find you must have/
if you really want to. You are not then distracted
by something happening next to you;
you are deeply everything.
If you find a transformation
in your mind/ a thought. Do you know
most people/ is something
put together by the mind.
Can everything on the bank/
crying you to find/ that you go beyond/
after all what is it that we all want.
Whether we all want to be/ we want to be
doing all the little things we like to do.
As we seek having these things,
we move onto something else.
I must be happy/ from the world.
We join to be happy together/ you
understand what I am
talking about. When you make yourself
part of your desire/ and acquire
some society/ they have all there is
to find. You see you have/
but sooner or later it becomes
the things we know. The kiss is followed
by everything withers. You must find out
this part/ when you are striving for it.
I can put what you have/ you are not/
you are not seeking it. When you are an effort
that requires trying to become/ somebody.
Something to be achieved comes into being

when you're striving/ and you are no longer
somebody; it is there timelessly
to everything that is happening.
You have to find out how
to free the mind of all fear.

LIQUIFY

The propaganda poster of a blond gorilla says *we dying we dead we dying we dead!* Each person that hears it for real feels something, but where do you place the something. I have a crystal box/ death. What of the sky, it looks dead. What of the white skin, it looks dead. What of colors just skin, just look sky dead look sky dead colors skin. I prop up my utensils so as to begin my meal. Things are just this way, race is just a sentence. No motion in the bones, no poverty on the white horizon. Only trash bones and pigeon seats full of sky box tears, dead sky box skin painted on the dead window box. The rote path towards a dumb forest a dumb forest with plain light.

SOMETIMES U DO UR BEST WORK WHEN U GOT A GUN TO UR HEAD SAYS A MAN

Style is important to interrupt
the ideas u already had about us.
Usually, I don't practice invisibility
with musings of other lives.
But I did once place Christmas lights
around my body and sit on a pee-
stained floor and watch unguarded
people busy time with thoughts
of colliding into the individual
planets on the ground.
The cold is past the lawn now, into a million
building halls. Men are straggling the sides
of my lawn chair, making the sun known.
I watch them with unknown hunger,
and unknown bliss. How the backside
of fame is always zipping up
the work we made with our hands.

As if the currency you keep is gathered
from working directly on a product.
Are you the product or is the product you.
Large gateway houses peddled
up to with the means to get in
to the home and cleanse the bar
of soap with a mouth, a pitiful,
unfed mouth. Don't say poor
or poverty. Don't talk about
history of/ without joy. And I—
I've memorized the past's
very bush-shelves, twine-paths,
dirt-sleeves. Don't ask me
about my/ Mother tasks
herself with building soap,
deft hands of history,
quick to work and to bed.

PAINTING THE HERMIT CRABS

*

I lie down on the clinical table, straddling the edges of memory
like a blotted-out horse, my legs still center part
ready to gape at the earth. After a good sleep on the trundle bed,
the pr*sident comes to a meeting with no arms and no legs.
Says he needs a Band-Aid. Says he hurt his finger. He comes
to the sandcastle, says *I'm making what I've always dreamed of.*
On a road trip, he is asked about his spiritual beliefs.
He likes god as a fixture hanging in front of his car window
or as Melania in her dress, discretely hanging
in front of his car window. The still ocean
has not forgotten the burden of its past.
When he sneezes into his arm-sleeve he says *I remember*
when that snot was just a young mucus. There is so much
mucus in the lungs these days. Not only
the monument's biggest nose but the ppl
themselves. The collective buildup.
The problem to breathe ocean clear. The phlegm.
Waiting for days on end to clear the throat.
No signs of change.

*

I pick a hermit out of the clear bucket and place it on my canvas.
As if I needed a reason to change their skin out of its original blessing.
Is the living ready to change as I dictate/ does it know
how much better it is to become what you are at someone else's hands.
In an ant farm the terrarium stays the same see-through body
from life to death. After inputting my life, I download a campfire.
I download a crab from the water's edge. In my hands, its life
is a slow breeze. Executing the task is only a moment's meditation.
I take a color unto god and exercise my power to make steadfast.
Have you ever heard the sound a cat makes when its paw is stuck in a crack.
It's like that. And then, godlike, I've made the thing new.

NEED TO BE NEEDED

I found a plastic star on the ground
like the one in your ear that night
we fucked and you told me about
the ppl who signed your walls
in graffiti stickers, how popular
it was to defy anyone's culture:
talk black or get hands, say
your prayers or breakfast goes
colder than that dead lizard
on the hot porch. Here's the thing:
either you pick a side or it picks
you. It's your problem—
to look into the closet and search
for something too high up.
Today, my hate is on an auto-renew.
A small hate soon answers
the demands of a lifetime.
I cannot dress up the fennel or make
myself leave sweaty pajamas:
this occupation needs my whole life.

HYPNOSIS

After Audre Lorde

Because the plant water yummy yellow drains dirt.
Because I am trying to pick up the dirt and dry the rest.
My dirty hands a murmur of the planted thing.
October morning finds the dirt outdoors, the water contained.
I account for what people remember
about the day they got it all cleaned up and packaged.
The evenings wander wet with mobilities
slandered by my normal bad intentions.
My hands wait at the throated ground;
a vacuum cleaner taking in hate everywhere.
Animal-bed hardwood floors I remember
driveway to driveway the plants strewn.
Hating you like never reaching
the lay-down grass. Hating you
for letting the animal indoors
like me. I remember finding
the lemon tree and asking
for a seat beside the living.
I name you both undone to time
and its power to divide the outside
with a honey circle on a far mountain
and the inside with its carry-on lungs.
The way you lose the breath
the more you go up the climb.
The puddle stains my mountain foot.
The gray woods walk with me
as I battle dirt and nothing.
On this patch of earth
there is nothing beside me.
No chirping merchandises.
No healing crystals.
No hotel pamphlet about the city sights.
If I could crawl out through
the air duct and surrender my nothing.
After all the days outside seeing blood
my hands cannot help but open
like judgement to the waiting room
of yesterday. I am inside

wandering these rooms,
godlike, wearing only a white cloth,
ready to decide
the patient is no longer ill.
Even as I enter the room to rest,
I smell the edges of the countertop
where we culled anger from its death,
taught it how to water a plant
and then go to the next room
and water theirs.
I am no longer
where I thought I was.
I cannot even bear to take
off my gloves and find my hands.

IF YOU GO INTO THE FOREST AND KILL AN ANIMAL, NOT ONLY THE ANIMAL KINGDOM AROUND BECOMES SHAKEN, BUT THE TREES ALSO

And I, having not a care but that of wandering the mazes my glass-sea fixations give way. As a seeping of sand enters my unfeeling hands, I fear the peripheral shadow that is not there. And if it is true, if it is really true, that it is not there, then I fear it more. I recognize the fear as truth. The drinking ligaments of green that hang upon the invisible thought. Recognize it as a thing I could claim, as a child takes to the caressing of old and common fabric, pressing it to the face with such vulgar passion and singularity, so as to make each stitching coalesce with the tissues of the cheek.

I give a laugh back to the mirror laughing at me. I give it a good hearty laugh of agreement, just as was instructed by the Sunday school teacher, whose pretty hands could always be pictured in memory to be holding a stack of white pages inked with the outlines of hair and smiles, for us to fill in with color. I liked to use the orangey-brown and the tealish-blue. And I hated that I had to share my colors because I wanted them, and I had them first, and mostly, I just only wanted my picture to be the only one that had that color that I liked best, because then it was easy to say why I won the

coloring game—which was only secretly a competition—and was only really a competition if you won, or if you lost. I knew I won because I had that feeling where you just sink into yourself and see all there is to know of anything. And the way I put teal down onto the line which bound the sea on the page. Or, for that matter, not only is it that the end gives nothing of delight, but the comings to, the crescendo, the drawling of the notes within a pre-fixture of pleasure, have themselves been all but a terrible gathering of misfit characters, awkward in their lonely outward gazes, as they try to

draw attachment to the figures of central importance. And as a fish has only the capacity of mind of its nature, of the water which nature casts it within to be fish, and I haven't the mind to think about how neither fish nor ocean can think of themselves as such—can order themselves as such. The awareness that the unthinking ocean cannot think it unfit to be what the fish is. I must know myself the complete victor/ the complete captor—as to be the thing that chases the wind and the thing that catches it back into the hands of sky. To win, I must be in the position of winners, in the huddle of waiting bodies, stationed pre-race, under a tent. Yes, I am ready. I am the fish. I am the ocean. I am whatever the name may be for the one to whom glory is received upon a shining tomb of perfectly stemmed flowers. And I cannot but be thankful that it will have ended. This thing I so long carried, so long *carried*. This thing—it was me—and I carried it. I'm outside in the sun now. Even the insects can think of nothing else but what sweat does pour out as they swarm in listless gray patterns about the echoing light.

MY DESIRE IS RED THIS MORNING

to separate the outside
from the in.
I can't yet tell the difference between
the iridescent scales of a leash
and my tongue forming words like foreign.
There was part of the dinner table
we used for things like yellow jams
and part we used for mesmerizing
ourselves with excess. It's so nice
to animal a yard with new stones.
The new fig branch is too small to carry
me back indoors. It never hurts
to ask for more blessings.
The microwave keeps reminding
me cellphone. It's always elsewhere
is the thing. The balmy heat reminds
me that window animals are out eating,
claying their feet into untilled earth.

I too am the animal indoors.
I have to unleash the indoor news
onto the unclean water elsewhere.
In celebration of the graves
of knowledge. Now it's a new year
and we can't help ourselves. Taking off
all our clothes like animals and pretending
we've never seen them before. I'm in the habit
of beginning to speak before I've listened.
The person I love just texted me "maybe."
I keep sending the yellow kissy-face emoji
when I don't mean to. It's hard to take
the news out the microwave and look
at it. *Never mind* I say to the river-
streams and animal-fish. Enough.
Enough enough.

RESTING PLACE AND OTHER SLOGANS

Community. Communeeeity. Communiii.
Communion. Commune. Commuuu. Comma.
Commaat. Commas. Commit. Exercise a right. Exercise your right.
Your right, roght, rought, your wrote, your rote, roate, rate.
What does community mean to the world outside
my limbs. Brush it off brush the excess down the drain.
Drain sink drain sink drain sink.
Push the excess outside. The perimeter of the mall carousel.
Bring the outside in. I'm running through the lawn outside
while the sprinkler fires fast. At the bottom of the hill,
we talk about how far or fast. The bottom is sinking in
is the stomach, is the middle, the center. The sprinkler daisy
or spilling fire hydrant transferring over to smiles.
An adjective can describe a place or a state of being.
Like I am not the wet water that hits my body, I am not
the yard I run through. I run through the yard, I run through
the wet street. The billboard parked at the edge of the street
keeps marketing a vision of what to know about the world.
If a world leader travels and is wet with divisiveness
but says it does not exist. If power can just say it does not exist.
If I can just say it does not exist. I'm pressing my body against
the foam on the walls, I'm going through it without thinking.

NOTES

The quote in the epigraph is from a talk Fred Moten gave called "Blackness and Poetry."

pg 32. The title "That which carries breath or the living wind" is a quote from Fred Moten.

pg 38. The title "A darkness invented by thirst" is a quote from Ocean Vuong.

pg 44. The title "The infinitely efficient body" is a quote from Milan Kundera.

pg 45. The title "And so we got to be for each other what the other missed" is a quote from James Baldwin.

pg 48. "Listening" is an erasure from Jiddu Krishnamurti's *Think on These Things*.

ACKNOWLEDGMENTS

Thank you to my brother, Davis, for teaching me about love, for making his life and his music love. Davis taught me what writing and living and loving were. I am blessed to continue his music in the best way I know how.

To my parents, thank you for teaching me all that is worth knowing. Thank you for teaching me about listening and loving. For being excellent listeners and learners. I am constantly learning from you.

To Stephanie, thank you for teaching me safety and home. I am happy to keep learning with and loving you.

To Rissa, thank you for being such a strong and wonderful constant in my life. I am so grateful to be able to depend on your friendship and smile. I love you.

To Elana, thank you for making this very thoughtful cover art and for teaching me about music and listening.

To Mateo and Estelle, thank you for being creative geniuses and constantly inspiring me to take more risks and be true to self.

To the AMAZING editors at Autumn House, namely Christine, thank you for all your hard and excellent work putting all this together.

To Terrance Hayes, thank you for selecting this manuscript and being a thread in the voices or a part of the tune that I am able to sing.

To Donika Kelly, thank you for spending time with this manuscript also and responding to it with love and tenderness and reality and vision. I am grateful for how your poetry touches the world.

To Alexis, Alan, and Rob, thank you for making thesis workshop excellent and helping me to have the confidence to speak and be heard.

To my first poetry teacher, Jeff, who listened and taught and opened up a sidewalk that I can keep walking down.

To Farnoosh, thank you for introducing me to the book *Think on These Things* and teaching me the power of attention and listening.

To Dolapo, thank you for telling me to enter this book contest and for being a friend.

To Eden and Briana, thank you for being bright lights, for being the closest thing to pure I know, for teaching me honesty and love.

To Josh, Jazzy, Tairou, and Terra, thank you for being genuine friends, particularly when I needed friends most.

To London, Lydia, and Eddy, thank you for walking with me even from afar. I love you in particular.

Thank you to the *Indianapolis Review* for previously publishing the poem "What sort of animal are you."

ABOUT CAAPP

The Center for African American Poetry and Poetics' (CAAPP) mission is to highlight, promote, and share the work of African American and African diasporic poets and to pollinate cross-disciplinary conversation and collaboration. Housed at the University of Pittsburgh, CAAPP's programming aims to present live poetry and conversation, contextualize the meaning of that work, and archive it for future generations.

The Center emerged in a 2015 brainstorming session between poets Dawn Lundy Martin, Terrance Hayes, and Yona Harvey, and was officially founded in 2016. Today, the Center is a space for innovative collaboration between writers and other artists, scholars, and social justice activists thinking through poetics as a unique and contemporary movement. In its effort to highlight, promote, archive, research, and generally advance the practices and epistemologies of African American and African diasporic poetry and poetics, CAAPP supports individual writers, artists, scholars, and others nationally and at a range of career stages and academic ranks. The Center also prioritizes providing opportunities for poets and artists outside of academia, in the Pittsburgh community and beyond.

ABOUT THE CAAPP BOOK PRIZE

Started in 2020, the CAAPP Book Prize is a publishing partnership between CAAPP and Autumn House Press with the goal of publishing and promoting a writer of African descent. The prize is awarded annually to a first or second book by a writer of African descent and is open to the full range of writers embodying African and African diasporic experiences. The book can be of any genre that is, or intersects with, poetry, including poetry, hybrid work, speculative prose, and/or translation.

NEW AND FORTHCOMING RELEASES

American Home by Sean Cho A. ◆ Winner of the 2020 Autumn House Chapbook Prize, selected by Danusha Laméris

Under the Broom Tree by Natalie Homer

Molly by Kevin Honold ◆ Winner of the 2020 Autumn House Fiction Prize, selected by Dan Chaon

The Animal Indoors by Carly Inghram ◆ Winner of the 2020 CAAPP Book Prize, selected by Terrance Hayes

speculation, n. by Shayla Lawz ◆ Winner of the 2020 Autumn House Poetry Prize, selected by Ilya Kaminsky

All Who Belong May Enter by Nicholas Ward ◆ Winner of the 2020 Autumn House Nonfiction Prize, selected by Jaquira Díaz

The Gardens of Our Childhoods by John Belk ◆ Winner of the 2021 Rising Writer Prize in Poetry, selected by Matthew Dickman

Myth of Pterygium by Diego Gerard Morrison ◆ Winner of the 2021 Rising Writer Prize in Fiction, selected by Maryse Meijer

Out of Order by Alexis Sears ◆ Winner of the 2021 Donald Justice Poetry Prize, selected by Quincy Lehr

Queer Nature: A Poetry Anthology edited by Michael Walsh

For our full catalog please visit: http://www.autumnhouse.org